A View from Tartarus

Michael Travisano

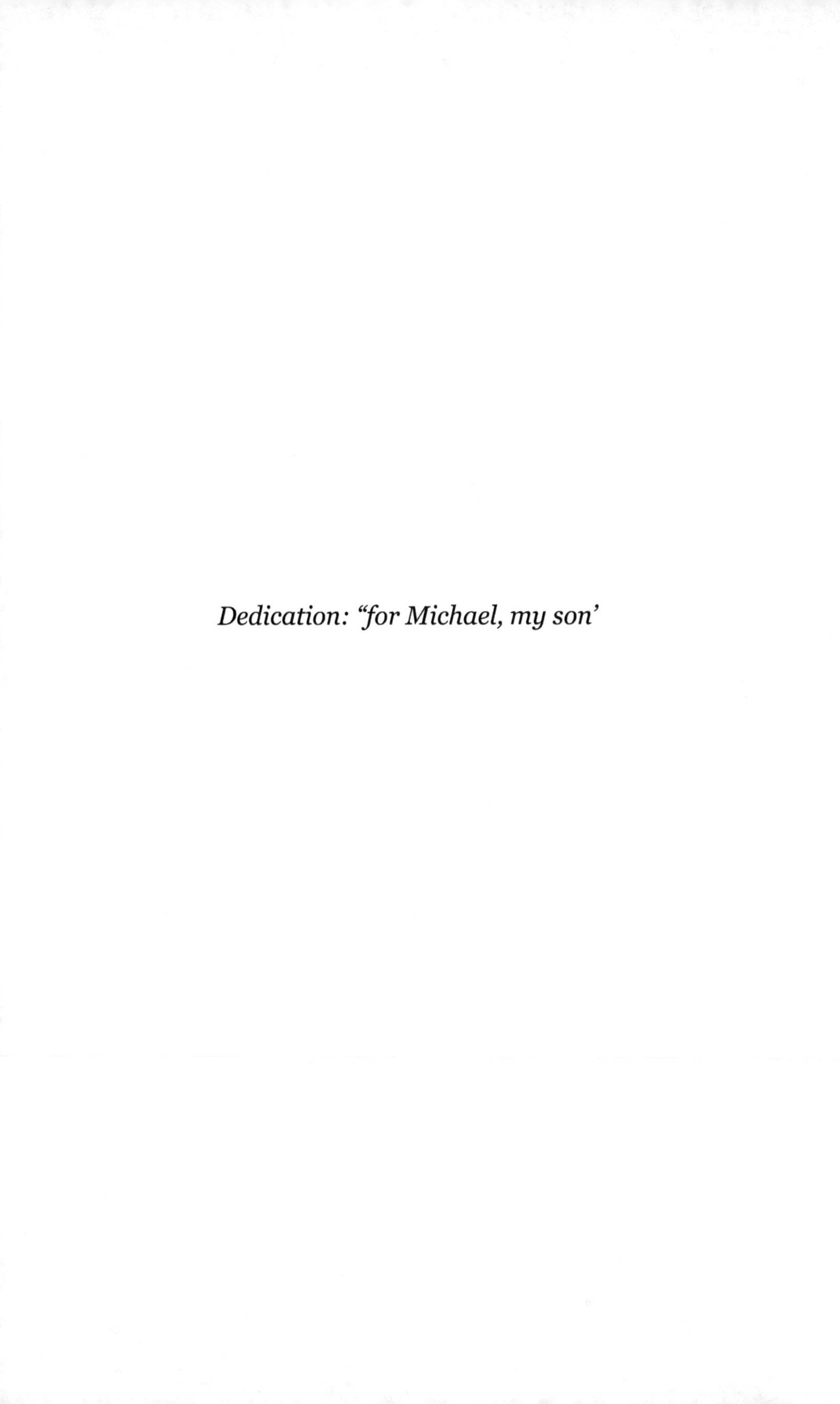

Dedication: “for Michael, my son’

Published by Human Error Publishing
www.humanerrorpublishing.com
paul@humanerrorpublishing.com

Photo credit: Elizabeth Sweeney

Front Cover: credit to my wife Suzanne

ISBN#: 978-1-948521-63-5

Cover design
by
Paul Richmond
and
Michael Travisano

Table of Content

Perhaps because it was so close to home, a sporting event meant to bring people together in the spirit of competition and camaraderie. Perhaps because it affected innocent bystanders, far from the arenas of war, or maybe it was a final tipping point in a lifelong litany of violence and senseless deeds, the poisoning of the planet, and the erosion of hope. The Boston Marathon bombing made me think as far back as elementary school, the Cold War, how we were made to fear the Russians. It made me think about all that has ensued since, and how there are few illusions left about peaceful existence. I spent three weeks writing 'Patriot's Day' and subsequently gathered other like poems. The collection, 'A View from Tartarus' is commentary, observation, reaction, to this 'lifelong litany'.......I'm 65 years old and passionate about language, what words can say and what not, about poems being part of the public discourse, poems bearing witness to both public and personal tragedy, that which any man may suffer, poems as evidence that we are not alone. I just wanted to get some of it down and maybe some of it out there. After the bombing, the Sunday Boston Globe Magazine, dedicated a page, a photograph of flowers at the finish line and a comment by Robert Pinsky, with a poem by Carlos Drummond de Andrade, that the event made Pinsky recall. I was disappointed, wishing, naively, I suppose, there were more poems publically available in the aftermath. We are caught and held in desperate times, no different, sadly, than our forebears, and there is, of course, always more to the tale, more that can be written. These poems are hopefully a mirror, some of what was saved in the long years. Given the choice, I'd hope they were 'important' poems, rather than necessarily 'good' ones...

May 2013

Lend Me

Lend me 20 minutes,
or an afternoon out of your life,
every other month or so.
I'll close the door behind you.
We will be safe, un-disturbed,
and I can show you the room
where the walls are white
and covered with words.
Words constructed out of hope,
slashes of black paint, thick and thin,
words meant for you.

You can examine with leisure
and read what you wish.
All sorts of tales, finished pieces,
bits of remembrance.
Words of love. Anger.
Wanting and waiting,
loss and survival.
Words about the seasons,
the stars, about home.
About the sand at the shore.
About daughters and fathers gone,
and mothers' still bearing
the burdens of their sons.
You can read about the black dog.
About vigilance, chaos,
and careful watching.
Can learn about the crazed solitude
he and I managed,
and how some secrets must be kept.
You can find out to what use
a good fire can be put,
and what is taught by the trees

You might even hear
what a heart might say,
given a voice,
and freedom from worry.

You can read all kinds of things
and know better,
how sleepless nights were spent
among the war dead,
when no one was here
to help identify the remains,
all of us caged by winter.

How, with age, spring is slower to arrive
and more anticipated every year.
Then leashed to dark summer nights
stumbling in the heat, calling out.
Falling, at last, everything a little sadder
when the leaves turn. Watching, wingless,
as the geese leave.
The story is here.
What I was made to wonder,
when I was sure of nothing.

But choose wisely, assuage your interest,
get your bearings about how I lived,
when you were not here.
Because after a time
every line will be covered.
Every important word whitewashed,
brushed under another coat of paint,
after which,
the ranting and writing
will begin again.

From There

A few words said in a rush
will not often suffice to convey the feeling
or finish the story I want you to hear.
The full explanation of the wanting,
when it is close, clutching and insistent.

Time, slowing to a crawl.
Trying to manage a few moments
and touch deep places,
recalling a tale I tell myself
on long winter nights
that finally deaden our voices
and keep us apart.

Word has come
from the distant mountains
and over the great oceans.
The sun was seen!
Meandering far to the south,
shining over open lands,
keeping flowers and forests
nourished and green.
The natives say Helios is tired,
and less willing to provide light
for the affairs of men.
Look far, even the galaxies
are moving away from us.
We must wait with our wishes
until the thaw, when water again
will run over soft earth
and it is safe to hope again.

After all our promises have failed
the landscape of the heart changes.
Out beyond where our memories
come to rest, there are promontories
and stone towers.
It is from there I will call to you,

from there.

Poem Purgatory

I imagine I'm preparing
our last supper on the ridge,
cooking a slew of onions, flaming the meat.

If we leave tonight,
we'll need to stop for gas,
then we're gone.
As far as we can,
no more distances,
nothing left to measure
that would make a difference.
Just our own gravity,
the pull of skin, eyes,
hearts and hands,
the hard breathing between kisses,
a vow unspoken but loud.
No words, images, or arrows
are required. Everything,
is in the touching, the blood storm.

Intent on a simpler life,
one thing left ---
our common ground,
ignoring the rest, trusting no one
and not listening to the news.
Just wanting the best parts now,
lying beside, holding hands,
while we talk about nothing
and settle for love.

Like we do, the words and wine
fit together well. But it takes more patience,
a stronger will, when you are absent,
it's blood simple ---
stuck, on what might be, you,
always within my best reach,
then, everything would have a part,
in the saying of love instead of lament.

Always so far behind
the plight and paradox,
because at last, desire ripples
and overflows our poor boundaries,
washing away most all
of the struggling words,
the ones we worked so hard for,
the ones it took so long to put together,
the ones we wanted to shout to the stars.

When the rant is done and the pen still,
there is an un-easy peace.
Able to walk away
and maybe sleep better
before she finds me again,
meeting in an old place
and feeling it for the first time,
thrilled and terrified once more,
writing such poor poems
and loving this hard.

for Suzanne

The Wolves of Solitude

Come sit,
I will share the silence with you.
Here by the fire there is no wind.
The smoke is clean, rising peaceably
through pines protecting us,
sheltering us from the passage of time.
It is another day without a dance.

Wanting comfort, we need not divulge secrets.
Nor private wishes we might be saving
for someone special,
someone we might yet know as true.
No one is coming, no one looking for us
to explain anything.
Let's wait until there's so much silence
it finally explodes into a great
and unexpected adventure,
leading us to willing arms,
or on a long trek to the bottom of time,
where our names and our stories will never matter.
Or to high mountains, far from home,
where we are forced to forget
who we are.

Let's not worry so much
about finding The Way.
Let us be grateful
for any human touch,
granted and given
to stave off
the wolves of solitude
when they are stalking the night.

The Shining of Important Stars

There's not much I wouldn't give for silence.
For long relief from the noise of the world,
the warplanes and sirens,
the distant cries for help, repeated and
unanswered, night after night.
The incessant drone of cars and trucks
beating down the roads,
rushing to the next place of our doings,
adding to the rabble and throng,
the throbbing of Earth,
moaning from our terrible deeds.
The cracking voices asking to be saved
from the cold hours of struggling lives,
asking for shelter and food,
their pleading now audible
for anyone to hear.

Relief from the ranting,
the rhetoric of diplomacy
perfectly articulated phrases
meant not to offend,
while bombs and bullets
become the symphony of our time.

What if all there was to hear
were the trees conversing,
whispering to us of the sea,
of loved ones calling us home?
What would it be like
a world gone quiet?

Give me wind against the walls.
Bending and creaking the pines,
the footsteps of fallen limbs
on the roof, under which
words of love are loud and clear,
soft sighs, making me try

to get closer, up against you,
side by side, the same language,
all the summers of our lives.

Should there be good fortune
and if we're awake late enough,
the noise of the world will sometimes ebb
for maybe an hour, two.
Then, if we listen well and love hard,
the shining of important stars
can sometimes be heard.

Hard to Find

Maybe it's the lack of sun,
such heavy air, standing still,
cautious about moving, sweat forming.

Maybe the lack of good sleep,
or a lover beyond reach,
a bed with too much room.

Or perhaps the litany of senseless death,
the choices of the black angel,
the futility of solace.

Maybe it's the struggle for words,
the 'I love you' that tells it all,
every piece and promise.

Maybe the sounds of regret,
or the wine, the coughing
from too many cigarettes.

The distaste of random circumstance.
The inability to reason it out,
or the memories that stir.

Maybe because time is a trick,
a rueful by-product, a sagging weight
on slumping shoulders.

Maybe the unexpected phone call,
or an important message,
never received.

Or a singular truth never revealed.
A sin never reconciled.
A prayer never redeemed.

Maybe it's the poor listening,
the paucity of wonder,
the indifference of the stars.

Maybe it's the common thread
we cannot find, in the right to bear arms,
and the wrongs that result.

Maybe it's the songs
we don't play anymore,
every protest swallowed by fatigue.

Maybe it's the machines,
or the absence of the dog,
his empty space, the perfect silence.

Maybe it's the useless poems,
leaking out of a tired heart,
struggling to hope.

Maybe it's the barren morning,
the long dry spell, the poverty,
all the chances taken,

that today
makes forgiveness,
so hard to find.

Everyone says forgiveness is a lovely idea,
until they have something to forgive
C.S. Lewis

Lame Dogs

Only the black dog and I.
Living in this poor house,
stumbling to find our footing,
our place in the scheming
of a random world,
turning as it must.
We've been quieted,
unable to cover much territory.

Grateful then all the more
for love having time to breathe,
grounded and safe when she is here,
and sure of nothing when she is not.
Every venture precarious,
clear steps are not always possible.
Often hard to tell if we are forging ahead
or falling behind, if anyone is listening
to our tired tale.

We wait for the sky
turning its hopeful blue.
For the green of early summer
to swallow everything. Enough!
Of these soaking rains,
the grey deathliness above
threatening to put an end to us,
to take away every hope
we hoped for hard,
late at night, no one here,
nobody coming, afraid and crazed.

What if it is too late?
What if we are too old?
What if too much time
has gone by?
What if there is
no remedy for our crippling?

Treachery

Miles of minutes
past the need for sleep
but I would wait
this long,
longer,

for one hour
of warm touch,
one true word
from her.

So see all my waiting,
please, this one time,
as a large act of love.
Then tell me about freedom
and if it would be so bad,
giving up everything?

Fortune is a treacherous thing,

today at the feet,
of a long-legged woman,
a woman once veiled, silenced,
but now walking down Newberry Street,
stopping at certain windows,
her shape evident in a sari that moves with her,
wearing a beret and one huge smile,
making hearts skip.

Fuck Wall Street.
I got no money for play,
so from November to May
it shall be scarves, sweaters,
soup and sex,
and I no longer care
what I look like
or how it seems,

living here in the country,
with no one as witness
to the madness that looms.

No matter.
The river is loud,
the trees thick.
No one would hear me scream
or hear the shot,
would notice if I were gone,
or dead in the backyard.

Freedom is a treacherous thing.

Jesse's Poem

The first duty of love,
is to listen.   Paul Tillich

A name becomes a life.
A face in a photograph
comes alive in your mother's eyes,
shaping the important details
through memories of wondrous doings
and how you were able to keep faith.

Sometimes when she visits,
silver charms jangle
from a bracelet you once wore.
Every one a story, a marker in time
of random circumstance, carried in her heart.
A few moments recalled
from your short life, fully lived,
and too soon gone. I listen.
With each new episode, I know a bit more,
what you did or said,
how you walked in the world.
I hear and begin to understand
the landscape of devastation
on the home ground of my lover's life.

Sometimes, her voice trembles in the telling.
Tears well as she pleads for your presence,
missing you, a grief without end.
In its weary silence my heart dies a little,
for this child no one could save.
For her mother, trying to be grateful
for what you shared, but always walking
the edge of despair.

Sometimes,
I catch her looking at the night sky
to find the star her child became.
I hear the loving words she speaks

into the great distance between what is gone
and what remains.
Then we wait the long night
for the one voice
she most needs to hear.

Burial

what if sorrows had substance,
and we could hold them in our hands?

Because she said
there was no more room
in her heart,

I told her I had
a shovel with a point
and would help bury
all her sorrows
way off in the woods,
help her to empty her heart.
We agree on the necessity
to put them deep enough,
far enough away
in the rockiest of soils,
so no roots could take hold.

We will wait I said,
it is almost dark.
The road will be quiet
and the river loud.
No one will see us
or ever know.

Ready to Sting

1)
Some things
rather done together
must be done alone.

There is no answer for it.
Our hearts bend,
accommodating the passage of time,
abiding its carelessness with our lives.
Enduring cruel circumstance,
we persist, mending and mending
the broken places.

The first fire of the year is lit,
soon, smoke finds us,
once again we do the dance,
moving round the circle of stones,
needing another place to stand,
trying to out-guess the wind
and so keep from coughing and tearing,
the damp pine slow to burn.

The black dog has settled in the truck,
his place of greatest comfort,
highest hope, every door open,
music, just loud enough,
drowning out the rushing cars
along the state route beyond the river.
Four songs, then out, sniffing some more,
lifting his leg as needed, on his loose patrol.
The sun is higher.
Another day in late winter,
no different than those before,
needing every morning hour
to make us warm.

2)
Some things done alone
are best not done at all.

Unless there is certainty,
a clear path of escape
and no one ever knowing.
No one finding out
who caused the damage,
whose vengeance was served.
No way to measure the carnage,
the amount of harm inflicted.
What a joy to walk away,
keeping such a secret!

Without particular purpose or prayer
I send smoke signals over Black Mountain,
towering in the east,
unavoidable out the back door.
The perfect neighbor,
never asking about the love stories,
or what the hell is going on down here,
never needing an explanation,

and though so far from the sea,
we are, in effect, burning the boats.

3)
Nights repeat themselves,
small hours on a slow march.
No one sleeps, everything's remembered,
random and un-important moments
from previous lives, a place or name,
something felt hard. Seeing faces
I have no need for,
no particular wish to recall.
I take up the shade
and turn around on the bed,
face the window and look far,

at the moon's last quarter
casting soft shadows in the yard,
at Scorpius,
poised in the south and west
just above the trees.

How grateful I would be,
having him come alive.
Ready if I beckon, to do my bidding,
Relishing in his undying loyalty,
his readiness to sting at my behest.
How busy we would be!

...the first thing he asked,
was if she knew the constellations...

A Better Night's Sleep

I'd begin with the monsters most prevalent.
Those who prey on the undefended.
I'd gather them up first
make them stand naked, row after row.

Then the torturers, the killers,
every heartless perpetrator of violence,
all the rest.

Then the poisoners of the planet
the uncaring, allowing our spew
to continue, not at all worried.

Next the thieves, the takers,
oblivious and without empathy
for their fellows, for the poverty
they create, for all they leave behind.

Then the politicians, the statesmen
and delegates, legates and lawyers,
liars all, posers for peace, for justice,
protectors of the general welfare
with so little concern for the people,
the poor, the helpless and hungry.
How sweet, to silence all the oratory.

At last, the warmongers.
All of you corralled, disarmed,
stripped of your medals and stripes.
Putting you together, separate from the others,
in close quarters, enemies all.
Saving you for last.

all the rest,

Those who mistreat dogs,
shake infants, judge by color.
Every advocate of terror,
the creators of fear,
all amassed, all accounted for.

I'd torch them all in a tick ---

to give the fox,
dead in the road this morning,
his life back.
His legs back, his rapid breathing,
his eyes that miss nothing,
his un-bounded spirit,
his knowledge of the world.

I'd trade them all in a trice.

I can't help picturing
a car full of kids, not well raised,
swerving to kill it, cheering
at the bump under the wheel.

For them, a slow, special death.
For the fox,
more running in the woods.
For the world, a cleansing,
and for me, a better night's sleep.

Crude Black Blood

The bile of the earth,
its deep viscous excretion,
now runs in our veins.
If cut, we bleed it.
Every day, in a distant desert,
young men and women
die for it,
while nearer to home
it spews into the gulf,
thousands of gallons at a time.

Our greatest terror
is going without it.
We'll give up anything,
anyplace that's in the way,
we'll drill and blast,
even create a war,
to assure our claim.
We are stricken with smoke,
our world, our only home,
fouled and under assault.

The moon-men saw it rightly:
we occupy a small,
blue and white rock,
the only color in an ocean of black.
And seeing it whole, they said,
it looked vulnerable, precarious,
in the starry background of forever.
Such a perfect truth
we need to learn quickly.

Soon, there will not be
enough good deeds.
Soon, helping hands
will be insufficient.
We suffer all governance.

Benevolent rule has mutated
into politics and politicians
who posture and promise.

Even those, (you and I?),
with no evil in our hearts
are guilty, passive partners,
our outrage stuck, silent.
Sometimes even our brothers
are not safe when violent deeds
exact their vengeance.
Desperation,
spreads new plagues among us.
Over and over again
always the same, always.
There is anger enough
and guns aplenty.
Our anguish so heavy
we are on our knees.

Voyager I and Voyager II
are leaving the neighborhood,
venturing beyond the last planet
into thousands of tomorrows.
We may never know
if they'll be caught and held
by Other's hands, telling who we are,
but so much of the story left out,

the terrible taste and sticky feel
of our crude black blood,
how it spilled and spilled.

Exsanguination

How thin do you think
can blood be spread
and still be recognized as tragedy?
As a sign of sickness.
A marker of our history.
A last stain, road signs in red,
mixing with crude,
with tears and sweat,
spilling into the pall
of lifeless irradiated seas.

Regrettably, Cronkite is gone.
Blessedly, no one's tallying body counts.
Remember? Waiting to see
if we killed more than they did?
Remember walking away
feeling good about the numbers?
Did you multiply them,
so the families were included?

Even now, long years later,
they recall his face,
how his voice changed
when he was excited.
How he so much wanted
to defend his country,
this next unknown soldier.
They never saw him again.
His little sister knows
more than the others.
She was the last one he looked at,
the last one he waved at
from the high deck of the ship
taking him to war.

How he pointed at her
and touched his heart.
And how she saw his shoulders sag
as he turned and walked away
into the rest of his life.

Resting Place

The sons and daughters
of mothers I do not know
are dying in a distant desert.
Thinking of it,
I want to cry and scream
but am terrified no one will hear
and what I would then
have to believe.
So I swallow a sorrow
I cannot explain
for families beaten, scarred,
because this next, honorable
and necessary war
brought its remains,
saluting and at attention,
to their door.
We're asked to believe
their blood was given for freedom
and for peace.
When the folded flag is handed
to another mother dressed in black,
sitting with a loneliness only hers,
one she will carry for all of her days,
she begins to feel in her breast
the dark pulsing of a broken heart,
her son's final place of rest.

Around her, and beyond,
rows of cold stones.
The world keeps turning
and tips some more.

Deception

Of fire and water and wind,
much, of course, can be said.
Fire needs fuel, a spark.
Damp mornings and wet wood
make things harder.

Every rush and bursting of water,
the great waves and surging tides
spread out and widen,
dying at last in the lowlands.
Fire and water have limits.
After a time their energy is spent,
eventually entropy wins out.

But wind has no boundary.
No valley will swallow it,
no mountains obstruct it.
Caused by a world turning
around a perpetual axis,
indifferent to the deeds of men.

When it is up, blowing and meaningful,
it will always find us.
Even if we are sheltered,
we'll hear it against the walls.
In winter, it makes us gather blankets,
demanding our notice and making us afraid.

Between November and May,
hunkering here in the north,
I only look at the thermometer
when it is in direct sunlight
it says 80 when it's 30,
and so on.

Groundling

Two eagles chase each other
over and through
the woods beyond the house.
Jetting between trees,
great wide wings
slap against the pine boughs,
not slowing them at all.
They crest again, racing over me,
I freeze, following their flight.
The world, the day, the hour,
made to pause,
as if we'd happened into
the bestowing of a small blessing.
Even the black dog
senses them above us
and is still.

Images and sound
held fast in the heart.
Long years later
they are easy to recall,
but now, only gratitude is left,
for brief insights
into the workings of the world,
how different it must look,
from above.

I felt sadness for my lack of wings,
and how this limits
the way the day may be spent.

Written In Stone

The grey slabs lay
like dormant beasts,
waiting for the age of man to end.
Remnant granite, forged before
the ape set his feet,
left behind by the retreating ice.
Some hidden, beneath the soft green
in the thickness of trees,
swallowed from ordinary sight,
covered over by aspiring bush and leaves.
It is early summer,
everything is vying for the sun.
They are stones that mark our time.

Never cut and carried away.
Not making it to the city,
not made into geometric walls,
neatly rowed and piled skyward,
lining street after street.
Not hoisted one upon the other
till they block out the sun.
Stones no one is interested in but me,
mere geologic oddity outside my door,
scattered along this rutted country road,
cut out and left behind, the remains
of an abandoned quarry.

Stones big enough
for children to climb over
and pretend they're on the moon.
Or some separate world
where they can explore
and search, for treasures
in the angular rocks,
found at every turn.

Able to believe any story,
relishing their bravery
before the unknown.

Yet even here, savagery is evident.
Knee-high by the roads edge,
across a thick flat stone,
a word has been written.
One of the root words
in the language of ignorance,
in the brutal syntax of hate.
A fearsome word. A terrible word.
A sad word, painted in blue block letters.

Nigga.

In Peru, Don Theo told us
how the mountains hold the energy
of our young sun, the infant Sol,
shining on a world yet without men.
He told how the aged stones
contain the first wisdom, the oldest vibration,
the natal heartbeat of our small world.

But here, today,
they are silent, telling.

Confession

Far to the south
below the equator,
distant mountains wait.
I recollect them without effort.

Led on horseback, silent,
in one enormous day,
to the other side of my life.
Looking far,
every horizon serrated,
the highest peaks snowy,
I went without resistance.

Long years later my voice
is harder to recognize,
scratchy and not as sure.
That of a stranger
who wandered into the present
where the black dog and I
walk the deep woods,
remembering old faces,
straining to hear again,
this time with exquisite clarity,
the good-byes
of all those who passed,
into, and then out of,
our lives, attached now,
to so little.

The far southern mountains wait,
I know. I hear them calling,
below the noise and hurry
of all these ordinary days.

Sometimes they are all I see,
and the one thing I crave.

Strange Notes

Love will depart,
but somehow manage
to find its way back,
standing at the door
late one night,
shoulders slumped
shrugging at me,
asking to be let in.

I now know it is faith
that leaves for good.
Indifferent to the sound
of our cursing, as truths settle
in those hollow places
we never get to fill.
This knowledge is important
but not comforting.
Late wisdom is not enough,
the droning ache in our belly
digs in, steadying itself
in the soft tissues,
where losses are felt.

Long years later
we understand more.
Having at last to reckon
the clear distinction
between how easy and wide
our hearts do open,
while beyond our best reach,
the hard world goes on.
Dubious faith,
ever more difficult to manage,
dissipates in a weary sigh.

No matter.

Every step of the way
we stuff our pockets
with all kinds of beliefs
and in the course of a lifetime
each in turn is pulled out,
and considered once more.
Many are crumpled and tossed away,
all the strange notes,
we wrote to ourselves.

Tilling

He is hunched, my landlord,
bow-legged, stiff in his walk.
He tips forward some,
but not dangerously.
With two of his sons
they have fretted and tinkered
with the roto-tiller for a week now.
It starts and dies.
They are not sure, just rust?
Or is a new part needed,
or maybe,
only a careful adjustment?
Simple as turning a screw
to provide the proper mix
of air and gasoline.

This morning, at the edge,
where words and hope meet,
I dig deeper,
but end up wrestling
with sentences and stanzas,
shrugging and sighing
because they're not quite right,
while father and sons
shout at each other,
ganging up on the wretched machine.

They get it running. It smokes and spits.
Encouraging each other in triumph
they tear up the plot of land
just beyond the screen-house
while I tear up another
useless piece of paper,
half covered
with scratched out words.
Every usual sound of morning
is deadened, scattered, windward,

taking with it,
everything I meant to write.

Because of Winter

If you come around, be careful,
soften your steps, lower your voice,
point no fingers.

Because years have accumulated,
and less is tolerated, less allowed
not the meat of life.
No longer interested in taking chances,
needing, more than ever, to know
I have a home at the end of the day.

Take care, it is February in the north,
when the loose edges of winter
become jagged, harder to manage
and every day starts with coffee
and cigarettes on the back stairs,
in the dark, marking stars again,
staring, awed at their distance,
saying their names aloud,
trying to keep up with stray thoughts
settling around sons and daughters,
here and gone, helpless,
while everyone sleeps, not able,
if it came to it, to scream,
and so the writing of poems.

Be careful, I am south of safety,
and it is easy to imagine,
doing bad things.

The cabin was small enough.
Not hard to find crazy,
sitting in the dark, walls close, cold,
measuring spaces and time,
enduring the lack of rhyme,
the lame dog,
what cannot be ignored,

what cannot be changed.
Careful, because now I write
in a small room. Tight, surrounded
by artifacts and remnants,
what cannot be given up,
struck with the knowing,
after long years,
how little of a life remains.

Because something taught long ago
must be learned again ---
the elements of fear, its cause and effect.
The facets of identity, truths sworn,
now wavering, the price of passion.
Because the demons and trolls
are coming round again,
violating the meager peace
of our small joys.

Because more room is needed
to stretch my legs and free my thoughts,
a long hall to pace in, when it is all
there is to do, a wide room to circle, over and over,
counting blessings, assuaging guilt,
folding flags, wiping tears.
Room enough to swing a sword,
to curse and swear without being heard.

Because a man, a father, can never know,
what he leaves behind, never fully understand,
the nature of his haunting, the terror,
beyond the stuff of blood
Because I miss the dog,
and that particular friendship
two humans cannot have.
Because there's only so much reach,
to an old man's arms.
Because I never get enough sleep
and am tired of being tired.

Because everything is sometimes.
Because I can only squeeze
a few good words out of the silence,
and there is so much more to say.
Because anger is etched in the air.

Be careful, winter's been long,
keep your questions simple
and ask them from a distance.
Kiss me like you mean it,
keep gratitude close and be ready,
to give everything else away.

Salvage

It took a good many lies
to become an honest man.
It took sixty years
and all manner of foolishness.

It took a lot of ranting,
mumbling and rambling
to speak particular truths,
because plain talk was so difficult.

It took a stubborn heart
to lose all the love
given or granted
in all the long years.

It took all that love
to be grateful,
for stolen, sunlit moments,
when you are here.

It took a lot of miles,
a lot of unsteady steps
to catch up, to see the sky
and find a home ---

where I need not worry
except for the wind,
that it is November,
and how long nights loom ---

in which I will wait for you,
always.

Meaning Words

Hours spent.
No one knows.
Crossing out words,
putting in new ones,
working the ragged lines
torn from angry cloth.

Out the high window
one crow confidently saunters
into my line of sight.
His easy movement distracts me
from changing a verse
closer to what I hear.

Like all crows
his attitude is knowing.
He is capable of flight,
and so need not ever,
worry over men.

Today,
distances are suffered,
every inch, mile, minute,
every line and the next.

I'd barter with that bird,
trade all the meaning words,
every blotch of ink,
for the use of his wings.

Code Blue

This is how the world works ---

Sorrow arrives with two teenagers,
tagging along, hitching a ride,
doing the town with them.
They do not know.
There's no warning
as they pull into the yard,
the sun high, promising everything.
Sweet whispers pass between
my true love and I,
we have nothing to do,
blessed under bright light at last,
a day of our own, agreeing,
how these are the moments
we live for and like thieves we revel,
counting our gold.

They are friends these two
this boy and girl, neighbors,
without promises to keep.
The boy is asked about his brother,
my lover embarrasses him:
"If he was of age
I'd have the hugest crush!"
The boy smiles in understanding,
"He's a good kid..."
He wants to say more
but can't, not to an adult.
He grunts his love
and voices a wish,
willing only good things.

Then, with that casualness of a child,
always such a surprise, he tells us today,
his brother's damaged heart
is being repaired.

I can almost see it,
stilled and splayed
by a steel knife
in a stranger's hand
under cold light
at a far city hospital.

The sun goes on,
not even a shrug,
not knowing what has happened,
this sudden strange turn
where we all have met.

This is how the world works ---

A message comes, wireless,
to his tiny phone.
He is like a lamb, this brother,
who does not know
the wolves are near.
Circling himself aimlessly,
his whole body shivers
before something too big
to get himself around, turning,
he asks, "What's a Code Blue?"

Now the day begins to shudder,
because we know, she and I,
know what this means
and how it can end.
Carefully we encourage him,
"Call your parents"
trying to keep our voices innocent and safe.
By text he is told 'come tomorrow.'
We press him again, softly,
call now, please call them now.

How it works is ---
even the perfect days
will have lives twisted in them.

No one can long escape.

Every grateful thought
or warm-hearted hope
is finally rendered useless
by grievous offense
and no prayers are ever
powerful enough.
A boy I don't even know,
has a heart ---
which may not start again,
may not begin his life again.

On the greening lawn
I mumble "Jesus Christ" over and over,
only just keeping my bitter anger hidden,
wondering again,
there's a God good with this? Is this
what we are supposed to believe?
A mystery, we're told,
not for us to understand. (their most convenient tenet)
Some divine necessity needing to be exacted,
or is he simply not paying attention
to such a small life,
so Lucifer can get a few licks in,
gets to draw blood, this warm day
in early spring, the sun oblivious.

The boy fearfully hopes,
mumbling as he leaves,
"He's a strong kid, he'll be O.K.",
his expression,
and compliance with the world,
unchanged, back on his dirt bike,
he motors away,
unaware of what I know,
what I have learned
in this chance meeting.
This may be the day
he will lose a brother.

This is how the world works,
even on glorious days,
and I don't believe
the sun ever cares at all.

Valiums & Vicodin

The valiums and vicodin
are because we are desperate.
Willing to swallow anything
if it eases the pain of bones aching
or memory stirring, stinging.
Of words un-willing to gather
and so be put to paper,
of empty arms reaching,
trying for a true love.

The wine is because
it diminishes the noise
and numbs the insistence
of the outside world,
the persistent calling
to order, purpose, reason.

Stumbling in the daytime
is not so bad, no harm done
if one is home alone and need only
manage the stairs,
find the bed, and sleep it off.
Waking in late afternoon,
forcing fluids, out of sorts,
thrust, un-willing, into another day
half-way gone, having to decide
where to be, what to own
and what needs attending.

Because after enough turmoil,
so sudden in youth, or that which
builds with age, after enough time,
with each succeeding insult,
each piercing circumstance
we are helpless to alter,
the muscles of the spine
are pulled taut,

and those of the heart
stretch thin. Before long,
we'll look anywhere for relief.

The pills are but accomplice,
because we're running for our lives,
wanting a great love,
wanting the hurt to stop,
trying to become invisible,
un-scathed, asking for amnesty,
and a bit of mercy,
in the landscape of the heart.

The valiums and vicodin
are protection of a sort,
a sordid medicine,
so nobody gets in,
no calls taken,
no promises revealed,

the only desire left to be left alone,
so you and I might embrace
what small joys remain,
though sometimes
they are hard to sort out,
when we're rushed,
assaulted with images and noise.
A little quiet is necessary now,
taking a long look, a step back.

Life is late, my love,
it would be enough
to lay down next to you,
and close my eyes.

Dirty Rain

Sustaining hope
is harder and harder
to manage.

The point of safe return
from our voyage
is far behind.

Oceans rise around us
walls get higher
soon we will not reach,

standing on every
last bit of truth
will not suffice

to see past
the next calamity
the next rocket red.

Kid on a corner dead,
one more innocent
who got in the way.

We look up,
no more stars
just dirty rain

and seas cresting over
our noble ramparts
washing everything away.

Today on Cable

Today on cable,
searching for diversion,
I saw Alabama policemen
beating black people with sticks,
1966.

I saw rockets erupt
from sleek ships
deep in the sea,
meant to defend,
carrying death to all,
every living thing.

I saw Kennedy's head
jerk forward and spurt blood,
saw her trying for escape,
saw the stain on her pink dress
and remembered being twelve.

I heard the wild bats again,
flapping their purgatory
over the tall pines
I thought would protect me.
Felt the fear again.

Where cast your lot,
chance, or fate resigned?
Or look to find
an answer in stone?
To die together or alone?

Today, at the only table,
a cold lament settles,
bending my head in prayer,
looking for answers,
writing down words
as they spill from the heart.

Wild Bats

The real 1960's began on the afternoon of November 22, 1963... It came to seem that Kennedy's murder opened some malign trap door in American culture, and the wild bats flapped out.
Lance Morrow

November waning, home alone,
most of the leaves brown and fallen,
age, not hard to measure.
Because I know, have sat and talked,
with people who do not remember
the day Kennedy was shot.
Don't know who Jack Ruby was,
don't recall Cronkite's solemn reporting,
or Lyndon's look of bewilderment,
right hand raised on a plane in Dallas.
Or how he would later escalate the war,
making us poorer, the smell of fear
on the wind, carried everywhere.
Didn't hear the gunfire at Kent State,
terrorism on home soil,
long before it had a proper name.
Often they'll smile or nod in ignorance
when I talk of Lennon's premise,
left to wonder alone what might have been,
about songs never written,
and if love really is, the answer?

No understanding at all
about the origins, the birthplace
of our collective absence of hope
in a world on the brink ---
hearts ablaze and souls amok.
Hey, God, what can we trade,
besides blood, for a little mercy?
What can we offer, besides prayer,
for warm beds and food to fill us,
for serenity and safety under a new sun?

The wild bats haunt the night,
like us, blind and hungry,
needy beasts, and while they feed
I wait for another dawn, another winter,
sitting with the stars, the sadness,

how peace never had a chance.

November 2013

Patriot's Day

If only there were evil people somewhere insidiously committing evil deeds, and it were necessary only to separate them from the rest of us and destroy them. But the line between good and evil cuts through the heart of every human being, and who is willing to cut out a piece of their own heart?

Alexander Solzhenitsyn

In the sixth grade,
they made us hide under our desks
in case they dropped The Bomb,
a colder war, then.

Five years later they told us, beware,
'the Commies are coming.'
Laos and Cambodia would be next.
Press On! said our president,
thrust into his role on a plane in Dallas
by an even more eerie violence,
a bigger death than any of us, at the time, knew.
Push On! said the commander in chief,
who would not let a lost war taint his legacy,
a tall Texan was he, to the very end.

Ten years ago they told us, beware,
a tyrant was building and stockpiling
weapons of mass destruction.
Another president,
telling us how it was necessary
to find them, to capture this next madman.
And though the bombs and rockets
were never discovered, we were not deterred!
More soldiers, sent far from home,
protecting us and our freedoms.
More young men and women, sent to fight,
losing eyes and limbs, just like before,
losing lives and much of their hope

for an ordinary existence.
Once again, our hearts made to sag,
suffering a weary grief,
and wondering which was worse?

Coming home from a foreign jungle,
an un-winnable war, to angry countrymen,
peace-mongers, fellow Americans
spitting at you, calling you 'baby-killers',
not heroes at all, or, to return from the desert,
a different kind of patrol, but the same fear ---
where would death come from, where is it hiding?
This time, in maiming explosions, a new kind of bomb,
lurking in the sand, strapped around torsos,
believers, just like us, doing the work of their God.

Worse, I think, for the now
more mechanized soldier, Seal, Ranger, Grunt,
men coming home to nothing, un-noticed;
no protests and no parades,
grey, wasted, leaving pieces behind,
bits of sanity, fingers and feet,
now less sure of their duty.
We are at last, benumbed,
with body bags and folded flags,
with officers at the door.

The years mean nothing.
Medals and brave tales will not suffice.
The dead mean nothing,
because nothing has changed,
nothing was learned.
Like before, the enemy is faceless, ageless,
he is everyman; barefoot boys and girls,
angry brothers and sons, rifle-clad,
with an aim to make bombs, following their fathers,
filled with a hate we cannot name,
still it drives us, gives us purpose,
more lives, given for the cause,
patriots all.

Part of the anguish is arriving again
at the realization: the world will betray
a thing the heart believes,
any of the stone truths, carefully placed,
at the foundation of our lives.
Simple stuff, never realized: one world,
the possibility of peace, the good life.
How we are all in, and of, each other.

Wanting to be grateful,
because of our fortune, our fate,
our place in the two or three,
human stories that fiercely go on.
But those stories are now altered,
harder to prosper, to persevere,
to sustain a ray of hope,
for our straddling the line,
between good and evil in every man's heart,
harder then to choose, who to banish,
where to cut or make a stand.

More of the anguish
is how they make us afraid
and then call us to arms.
Bomber jet planes and the dearth of butterflies,
the continual spilling of blood,
in the never-ending war,
with no balm for the fear, not ever.
Sad hearts work harder to beat,
resignation begins to overwhelm the ramparts.
Bloodied flags in smoky red glare,
should not be our solace.

Tell George the weapons have been found.
Right there all along, in the souls of our fellows;
at small town schools and finish lines.
At a theater near you. Assault rifles abound,
three hundred rounds a minute what a rush!
Computer pilots and drones

delivering death at a distance.
Stupid men with smart bombs.
Evil, in its diversity ---
any neighborhood will do,
no premise exempt, no early warning system,
no midnight ride to warn us.

War Dead

Battles once loud, out in the open,
flags waving and God's best wishes,
have gone guerilla. Hands and feet
once slowed by swamp and mud
are now flayed by sand and storm.

Why are the reasons for more troops,
less clear? Poor memories of past wars
allow fear to accumulate, we are poor learners;
changing our tactics to suit our myths and fables,
every patriot justified, ever and always,
a most honorable way of death, dying for the cause,
truth a chameleon, reliant on and relative to,
every possible point of view, certain,
that peace is won in blood.

By day's dark end we are fatigued and dirty.
We smell of cigarettes and panic,
comforting our comrades in this soiling of humanity,
more wasted lives and senseless death,
left to identify the remains of all we gave up.

Empty wine bottles line up like war dead.
We are slaves to a silence no words can broach,
we are the benumbed stragglers amidst ruinous poems.
What would we write of it? First,
we must admit the inadequacy of any language,
no matter how grandiose, no matter how plain.
Imagination and intent skirmish after dark,
difficult to tell apart without the waxing moon.
The verses and passages, the pleas for peace
and all the manifestos of tyranny,
each bent on victory, each deserving.
Waiting for daybreak or some quiet time,
to put them on the page,
all the studied sentences dripping with hope,

thinking hard about just what rhymes with what anymore?
scratching out words and folding flags,
trying for some kind of solace,
trying to say and save all those things
never bound by words or won by war.

Debris

Head and heart ---

The relentless dancers.
Intertwined, struck from all sides,
one, the others fetch.
Not always agreeing,
or seeing the same thing.
No matter.
They hold hands forever.

Sometimes,
tales of their damage, their triumphs,
are made into poems.
The talk, the sum of their tirades,
their travail, the prayers,
those shared moments looking far.
The roaming, the resting, the rush.
Sometimes the most important words
are made into vows.

The poems are what was saved.
Recalled and written down
before the next storm arrives
to blur the landscape.
Before the next meaningful wind
blows through, before the birds leave.

Poems are men, women,
dripping blood.
Stubborn, silly men, women,
who endure much, witnesses,
needing to have their say.

In the long years,
some of them
learn about survival
and only a few of those
get out alive.

The Same

How can we look
at the wide world
and not despair?
How can we manage
to find hope
when even the small joys
are such a struggle?
I am tired of being tired.
The dog is lame
and so there is worry.
Love has run off
to haunt others,
leaving me the morning
with nothing to do,
so I'll remember well
and sharpen my knives again.

Wine has been substituted for tea
while Canadian Wheat Bread
has been made into toast
then coated with butter ---

and of course I am older,
things matter less,
otherwise, everything's the same.

Previously Published

Tilling was in Birchsong/Poetry
Centered in Vermont Volume II.

Publication Michael has been published in
Oberon, Astropoetica, VTFolkus, Aesthetica, Birchsong, From the Depths, The Best of Write Action, No. 2, Poetry Alive

Photo credit to Elizabeth Sweeney

MichaelTravisano was born in Providence R.I., 47 years work as an RN, voracious reader, fascinated by language, its evolution over time, what words can say and what they cannot. Intrigued by what might be possible in a poem, and that they should be part of the public discourse, a counterpoint to the op-ed pages, if you will, considers his wife a gift, not all the poems are about Suzanne, but they are all because of her. Varied literary influences, but counts William Stafford, Jack Kerouac, and Charles Bukowski as the foremost.

www.ingramcontent.com/pod-product-compliance
Lightning Source LLC
LaVergne TN
LVHW010107110826
845155LV00028B/531

* 9 7 8 1 9 4 8 5 2 1 6 3 5 *